DECORATIVE NAPKIN FOLDING
FOR BEGINNERS

Lillian Oppenheimer
and
Natalie Epstein

Drawings by Gwen Williams

DOVER PUBLICATIONS, INC.
NEW YORK

Decorative Napkin Folding for Beginners is a new work, first
published by Dover Publications, Inc., in 1979.

International Standard Book Number: 0-486-23797-4

Manufactured in the United States of America
Dover Publications, Inc., 31 East 2nd Street, Mineola, N.Y. 11501

INTRODUCTION

There is something festive about a fancifully folded napkin. The very sight of an array of folded linen among the crystal proclaims a meal a celebration; and when the waiter, with a single gesture, flicks the folds open and lays the cloth across your lap, you feel like royalty.

Not many generations back, napkin folding was a backstairs accomplishment that added luster to the appointments of the dinner table in private mansions. Nowadays it is virtually a trade secret among waiters in elegant restaurants, where large linen napkins are still used. There is, however, no reason why waiters should have all the fun. Anybody can fold napkins! There is not even any reason why napkins should be linen, or, indeed, woven cloth of any sort. Big, square paper dinner napkins work perfectly well. It is important that the napkin, whatever its material, be truly square, and not limp. If cloth is used, it should be lightly starched. For best results, iron out all the creases before you begin.

The designs in this collection of napkin folds range from very simple to moderately complex. The easy ones are in the front of the book. Do them first. In following the diagrams, remember that each picture shows you two things: what the napkin looks like after the previous fold has been made and what you do next. Work on a clean, hard surface and press firmly, so that the finished creation may be fresh and crisp—ready to grace an invalid's tray or a holiday table. The user will have as much fun trying to figure out how you did it as you had in the making.

ALICE GRAY

HEART

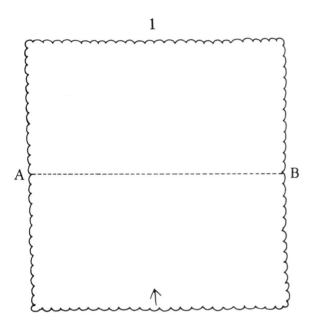
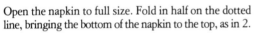

Open the napkin to full size. Fold in half on the dotted line, bringing the bottom of the napkin to the top, as in 2.

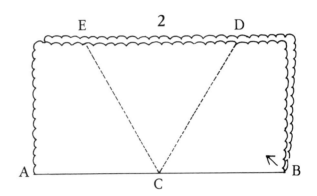

Fold into thirds along the dotted lines, picking up the lower right corner, as in 3.

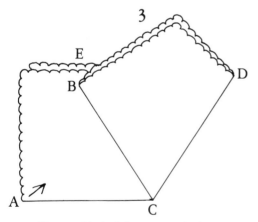

Repeat with the left corner, as in 4.

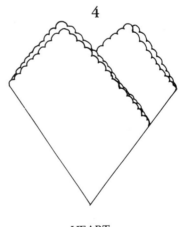

HEART

THE NEST

1

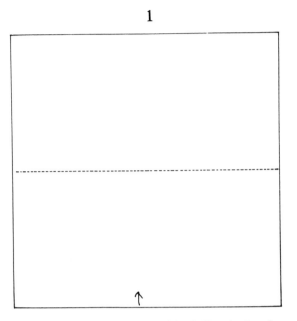

Open the napkin to full size. Fold in half on the dotted line, bringing the bottom of the napkin to the top, as in 2.

2

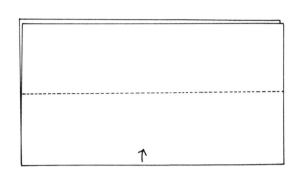

Fold in half again on the dotted line, bringing the bottom fold to the top, as in 3.

3

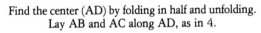

Find the center (AD) by folding in half and unfolding. Lay AB and AC along AD, as in 4.

4

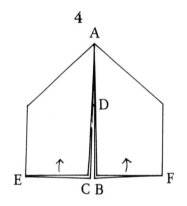

Roll up BF and CE to D, as in 5.

5

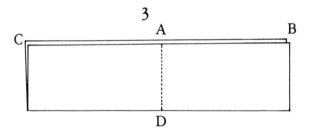

Bring the two rolls together in the front and stand up the napkin on the rolls with point A standing up high, as in 6.

6

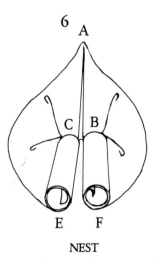

NEST

Place fruit, bun or flowers in the nest to keep it standing.

CANDLE

1

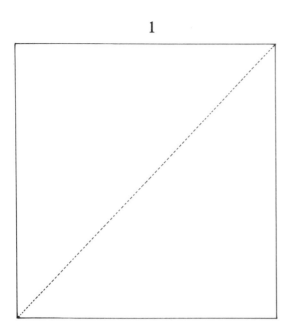

Open the napkin to full size. Fold in half on the dotted line, as in 2.

2

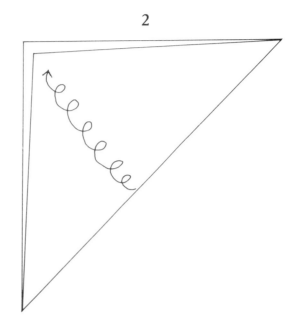

Roll up tightly from the diagonal fold, as in 3.

3

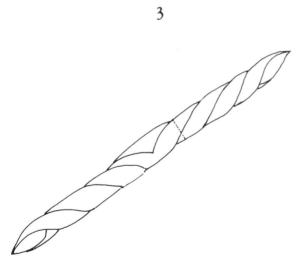

Fold on the dotted line, bringing points upward, as in 4.

4

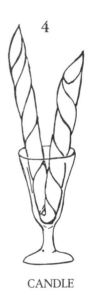

CANDLE

CORNUCOPIA OR CLOWN'S HAT

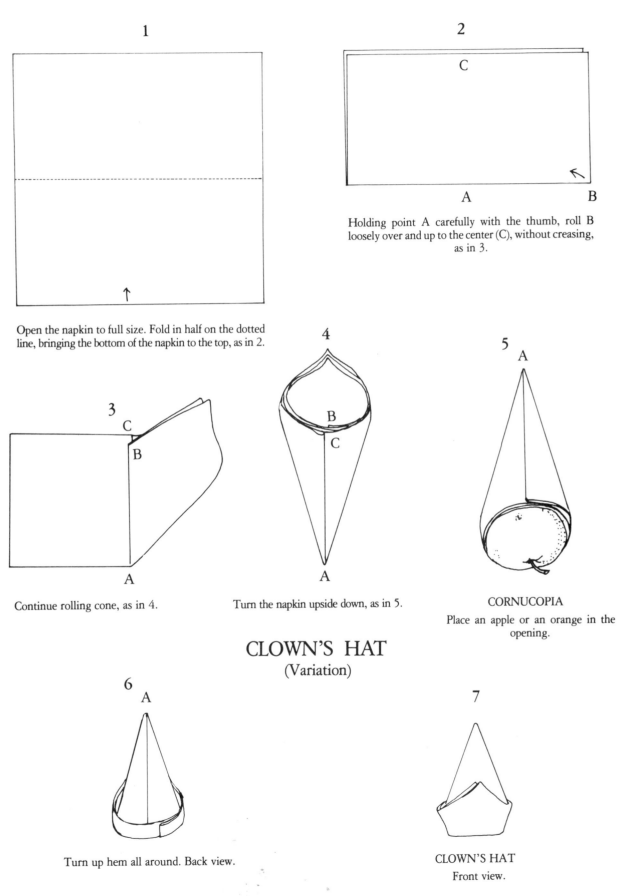

1

Open the napkin to full size. Fold in half on the dotted line, bringing the bottom of the napkin to the top, as in 2.

2

C

A   B

Holding point A carefully with the thumb, roll B loosely over and up to the center (C), without creasing, as in 3.

3

C
B

A

Continue rolling cone, as in 4.

4

B
C

A

Turn the napkin upside down, as in 5.

5

A

CORNUCOPIA

Place an apple or an orange in the opening.

CLOWN'S HAT
(Variation)

6

A

Turn up hem all around. Back view.

7

CLOWN'S HAT
Front view.

PLACE CARD HOLDER

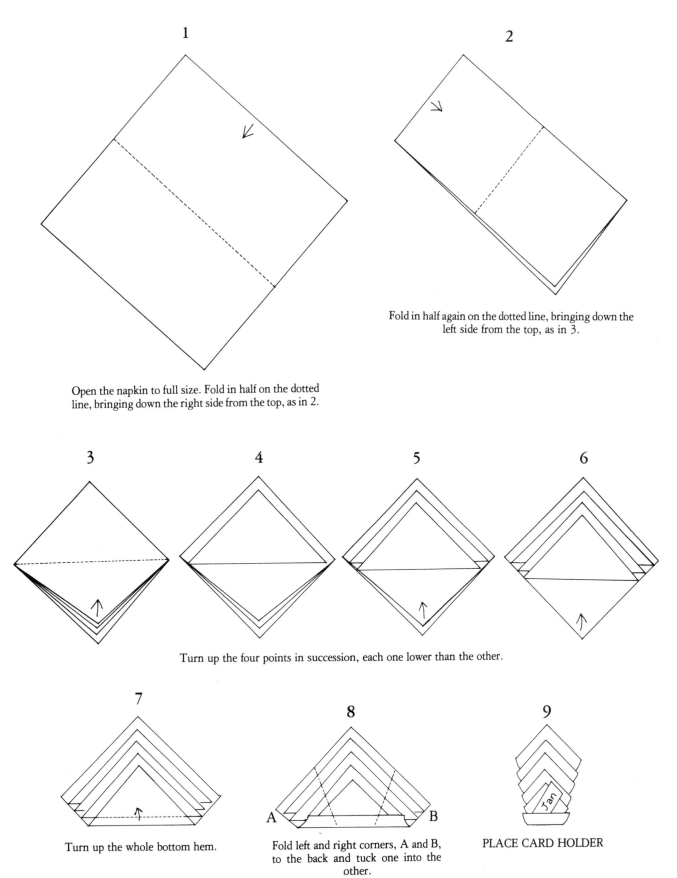

1

Open the napkin to full size. Fold in half on the dotted line, bringing down the right side from the top, as in 2.

2

Fold in half again on the dotted line, bringing down the left side from the top, as in 3.

3 **4** **5** **6**

Turn up the four points in succession, each one lower than the other.

7

Turn up the whole bottom hem.

8

Fold left and right corners, A and B, to the back and tuck one into the other.

9

PLACE CARD HOLDER

BOAT

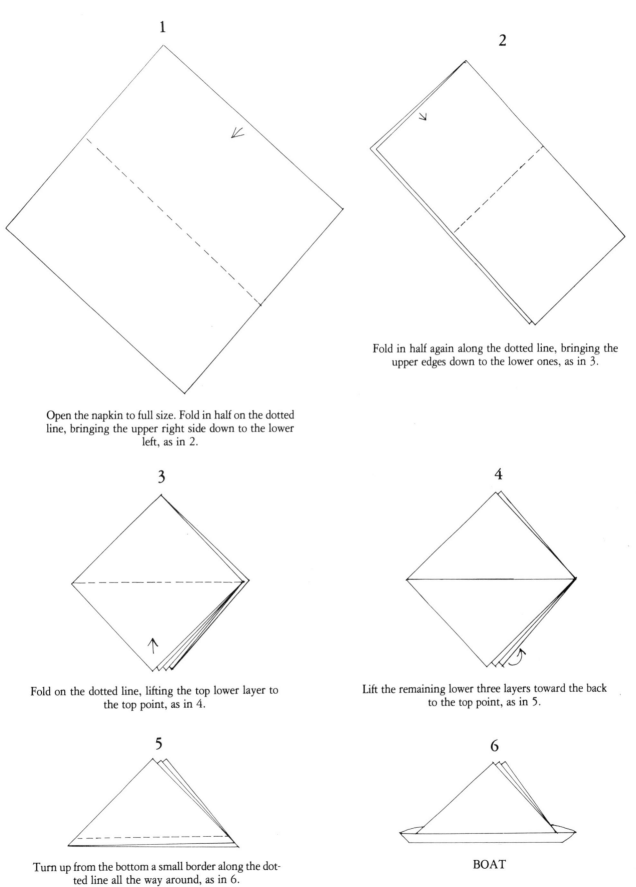

1

Open the napkin to full size. Fold in half on the dotted line, bringing the upper right side down to the lower left, as in 2.

2

Fold in half again along the dotted line, bringing the upper edges down to the lower ones, as in 3.

3

Fold on the dotted line, lifting the top lower layer to the top point, as in 4.

4

Lift the remaining lower three layers toward the back to the top point, as in 5.

5

Turn up from the bottom a small border along the dotted line all the way around, as in 6.

6

BOAT

SILVERWARE HOLDER

1

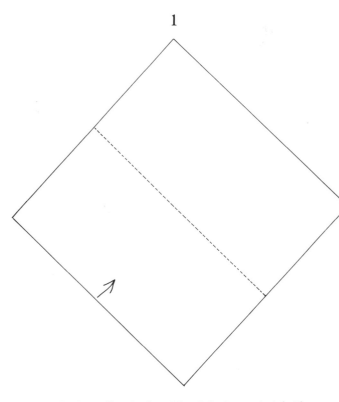

Fold in half on the dotted line, bringing up the left side from the bottom, as in 2.

2

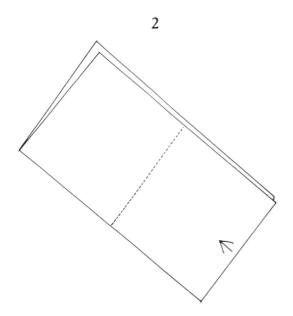

Fold in half again on the dotted line, bringing up the right side from the bottom, as in 3.

3

4

5

6

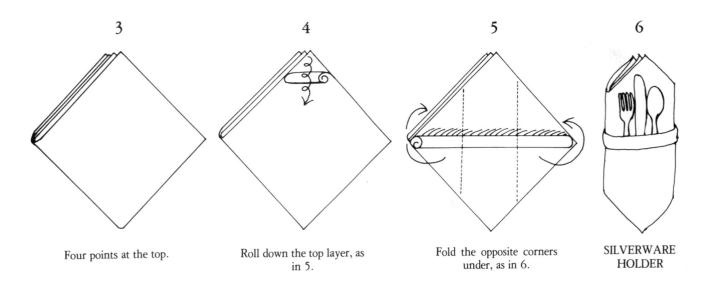

3 Four points at the top.

4 Roll down the top layer, as in 5.

5 Fold the opposite corners under, as in 6.

6 SILVERWARE HOLDER

14

COCKSCOMB

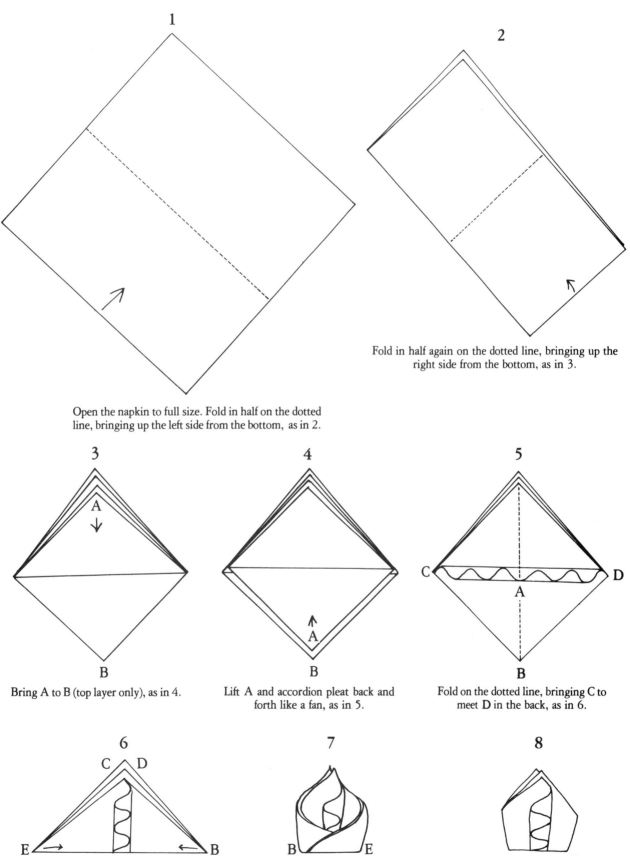

1

Open the napkin to full size. Fold in half on the dotted line, bringing up the left side from the bottom, as in 2.

2

Fold in half again on the dotted line, bringing up the right side from the bottom, as in 3.

3

A

B

Bring A to B (top layer only), as in 4.

4

A

B

Lift A and accordion pleat back and forth like a fan, as in 5.

5

C   A   D

B

Fold on the dotted line, bringing C to meet D in the back, as in 6.

6

C   D

E   B

Fold bottom BE in thirds, tucking point E into point B, as in 7.

7

B   E

Turn over for finished napkin.

8

COCKSCOMB

15

LOVE KNOT

1

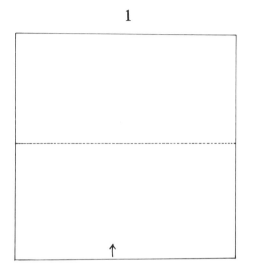

Open the napkin to full size. Fold in half on the dotted line, bringing the bottom edge to the top, as in 2.

2

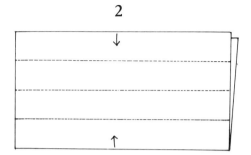

Bring the upper and lower edges to meet in the center, as in 3.

3

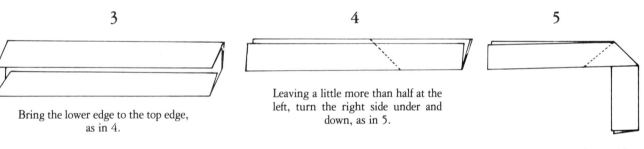

Bring the lower edge to the top edge, as in 4.

4

Leaving a little more than half at the left, turn the right side under and down, as in 5.

5

Turn the left side over so that its side comes along that of the right segment, as in 6.

6

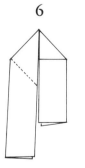

Bring the left side of the napkin over so that it is perpendicular to the other segment, as in 7.

7

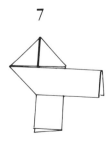

To tie the knot, lift the lower segment over the top one, as in 8.

8

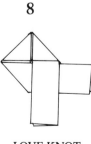

LOVE KNOT

FLOWER HOLDER

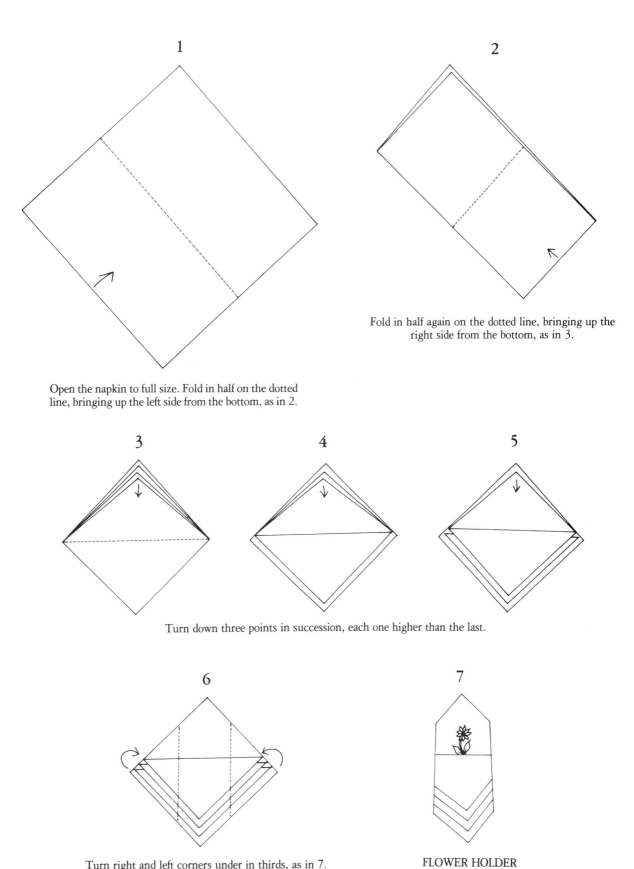

1

Open the napkin to full size. Fold in half on the dotted line, bringing up the left side from the bottom, as in 2.

2

Fold in half again on the dotted line, bringing up the right side from the bottom, as in 3.

3   **4**   **5**

Turn down three points in succession, each one higher than the last.

6

Turn right and left corners under in thirds, as in 7.

7

FLOWER HOLDER

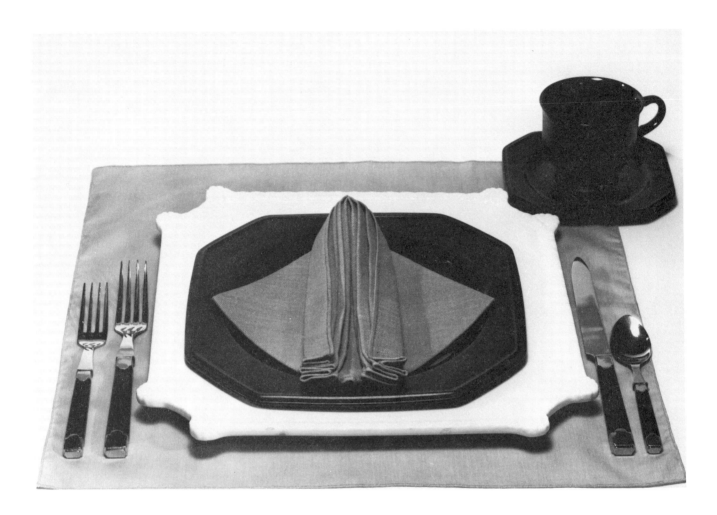

JAPANESE KIMONO

(Lace napkin can be used)

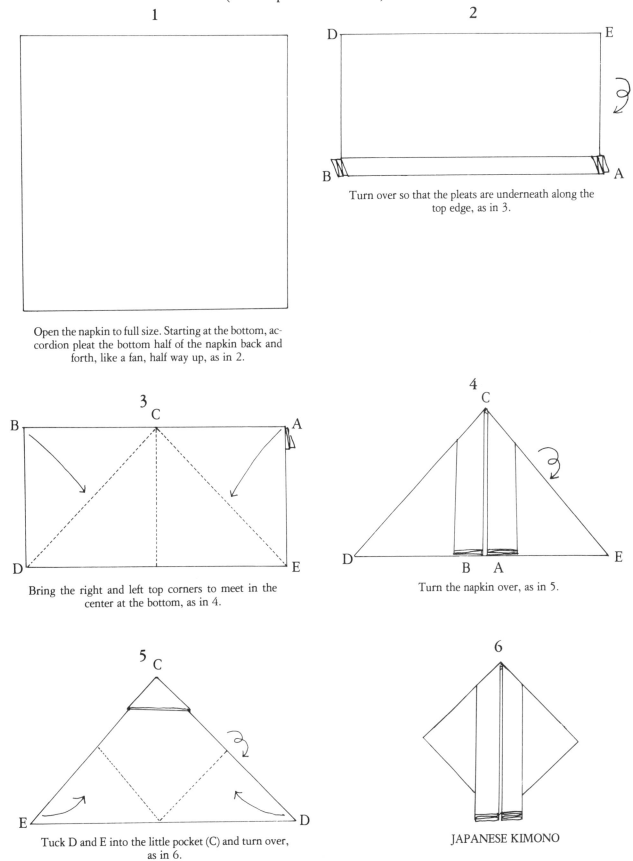

1

Open the napkin to full size. Starting at the bottom, accordion pleat the bottom half of the napkin back and forth, like a fan, half way up, as in 2.

2

Turn over so that the pleats are underneath along the top edge, as in 3.

3

Bring the right and left top corners to meet in the center at the bottom, as in 4.

4

Turn the napkin over, as in 5.

5

Tuck D and E into the little pocket (C) and turn over, as in 6.

6

JAPANESE KIMONO

ASCOT

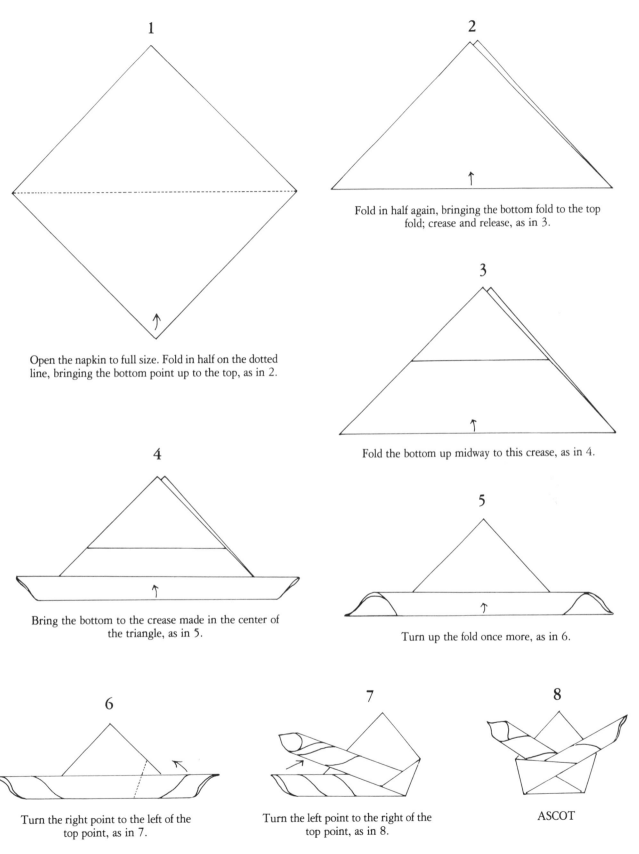

1

Open the napkin to full size. Fold in half on the dotted line, bringing the bottom point up to the top, as in 2.

2

Fold in half again, bringing the bottom fold to the top fold; crease and release, as in 3.

3

Fold the bottom up midway to this crease, as in 4.

4

Bring the bottom to the crease made in the center of the triangle, as in 5.

5

Turn up the fold once more, as in 6.

6

Turn the right point to the left of the top point, as in 7.

7

Turn the left point to the right of the top point, as in 8.

8

ASCOT

PEACOCK

(For napkin holder, use 7″ or 8″ stiff, decorative paper or starched napkin.)

1

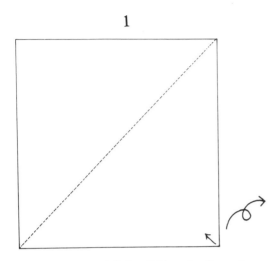

Open the napkin to full size. Fold on the diagonal on the dotted line, crease and open. Turn over.

2

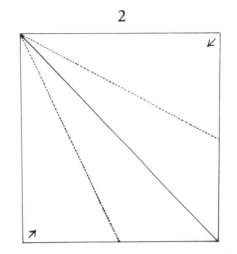

Bring right and left to the center crease to make a kite fold, as in 3.

3

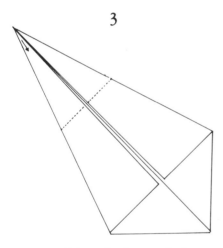

Bring point down, as in 4.

4

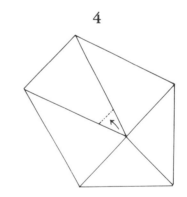

Fold the little tip back on itself for the beak, as in 5.

5

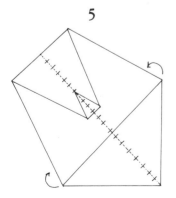

Fold in half to the back, as in 6.

6

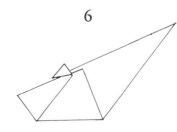

Pull up the neck and beak, as in 7, and pinch to secure.

7

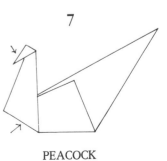

PEACOCK

CARDINAL'S HAT

1

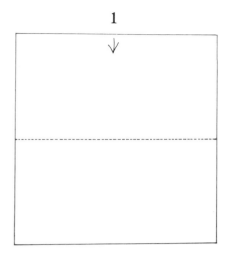

Open the napkin to full size. Fold in half on the dotted line, bringing the top of the napkin to the bottom, as in 2.

2

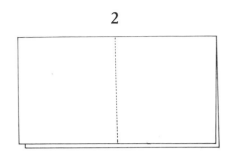

Find the center by folding in half on the dotted line; crease and open, as in 3.

3

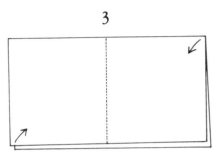

Bring the upper right corner down to the center of the bottom and the lower left corner up to the center of the top, as in 4.

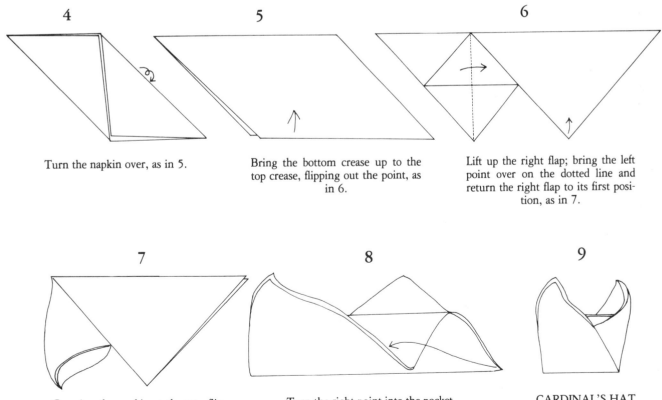

4

Turn the napkin over, as in 5.

5

Bring the bottom crease up to the top crease, flipping out the point, as in 6.

6

Lift up the right flap; bring the left point over on the dotted line and return the right flap to its first position, as in 7.

7

Grasping the napkin at the top, flip over, as in 8.

8

Turn the right point into the pocket, as in 9.

9

CARDINAL'S HAT
(Dinner roll may be served within.)

27

THE EMPRESS OR DUTCH HAT

1

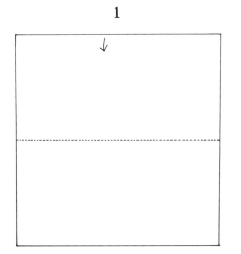

Open the napkin to full size. Fold in half on the dotted line, bringing the top edge to the bottom, as in 2.

2

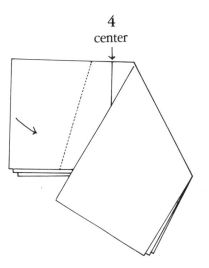

Fold in half again on the dotted line, bringing the top fold to the bottom edge, as in 3.

3

center

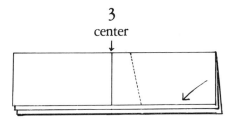

Find the center by folding in half; crease and open. Fold down the right end along the dotted line, as in 4.

4

center

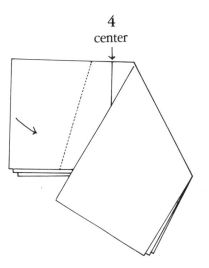

Fold down the left end along the dotted line, as in 5.

5

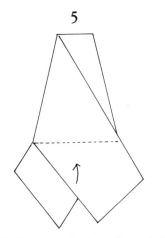

Fold up along the dotted line, as in 6.

6

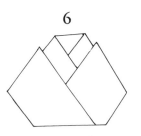

EMPRESS
Turn over the napkin for the Dutch Hat, as in 7.

7

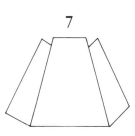

DUTCH HAT

SWAN

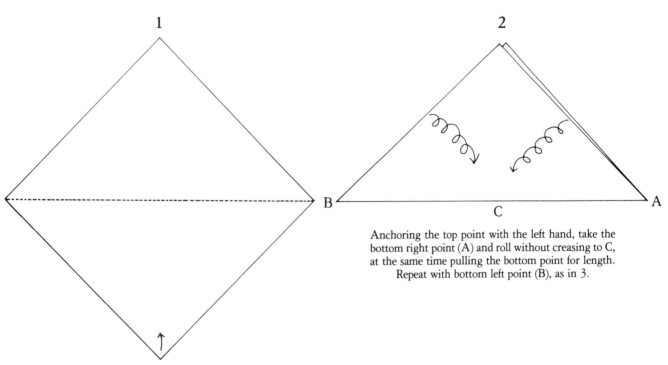

1

2

Anchoring the top point with the left hand, take the bottom right point (A) and roll without creasing to C, at the same time pulling the bottom point for length. Repeat with bottom left point (B), as in 3.

Open the napkin to full size. Fold in half on the dotted line, bringing the bottom point to the top point, as in 2.

3

Fold in half on the dotted line, bringing down the top point, as in 4.

4

The point becomes the beak; fold it up half-way, as in 5.

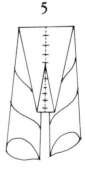

5

Fold in half along the dotted line, being sure that the beak and the neck are on the outside, as in 6.

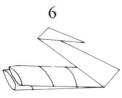

6

Pull the neck and beak up slightly, as in 7, and pinch at the lower point where the neck joins the body.

7

SWAN

31

AFRICAN BIRD

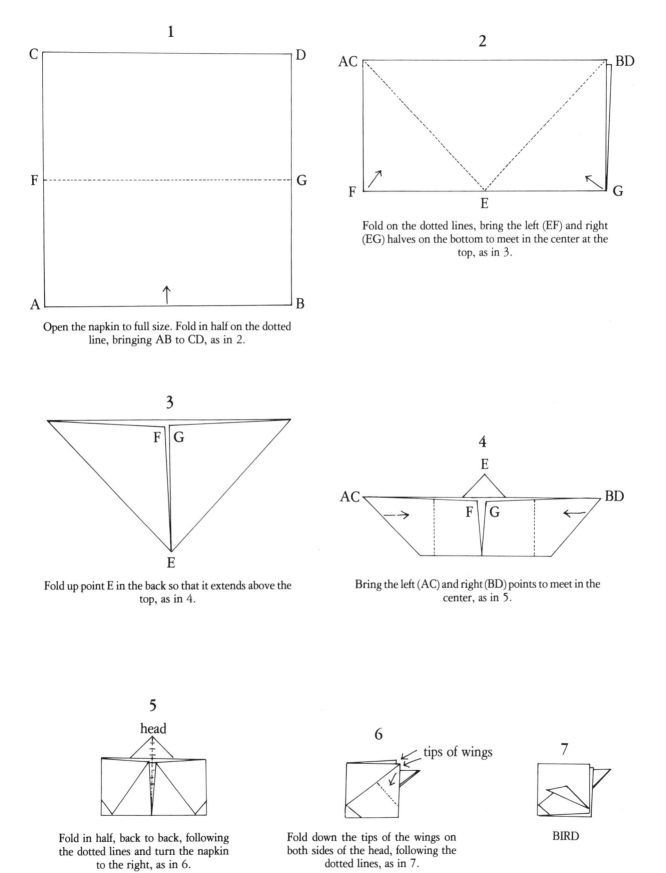

1

Open the napkin to full size. Fold in half on the dotted line, bringing AB to CD, as in 2.

2

Fold on the dotted lines, bring the left (EF) and right (EG) halves on the bottom to meet in the center at the top, as in 3.

3

Fold up point E in the back so that it extends above the top, as in 4.

4

Bring the left (AC) and right (BD) points to meet in the center, as in 5.

5

head

Fold in half, back to back, following the dotted lines and turn the napkin to the right, as in 6.

6

tips of wings

Fold down the tips of the wings on both sides of the head, following the dotted lines, as in 7.

7

BIRD

LADY WINDERMERE'S FAN

1

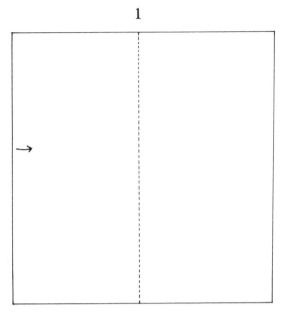

Open the napkin to full size. Fold in half on the dotted line, bringing the left edge to the right edge, as in 2.

2

Starting at the bottom, accordion pleat back and forth about two-thirds of the way up, as in 3.

3

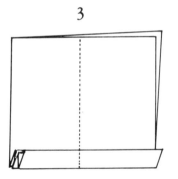

Fold in half on the dotted line with the accordion pleating on the outside, as in 4.

4

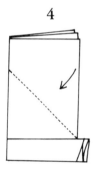

Fold on the dotted line, laying the right side along the accordion pleat, as in 5.

5

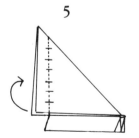

Turn overlap on the left on the dotted line toward the back; rest that overlap on the table, letting the fan open, as in 6.

6

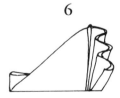

Side view. Turn for front view, as in 7.

7

LADY WINDERMERE'S FAN

BUTTERFLY

1

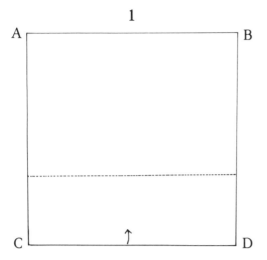

Open the napkin to full size. Fold the bottom third of the napkin up, as in 2.

2

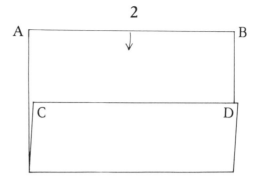

Bring the top edge to the bottom fold, dividing the napkin in thirds, as in 3.

3

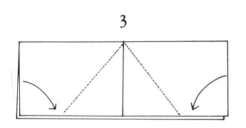

Bring the left and right ends to meet in the center, as in 4.

4

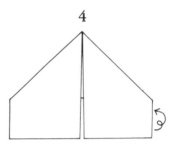

Turn the napkin over, as in 5.

5

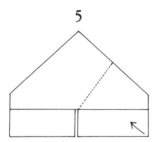

Swing the right flap over to the left, as in 6.

6

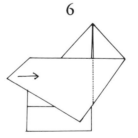

Swing the same flap over to the right on the dotted line, as in 7.

7

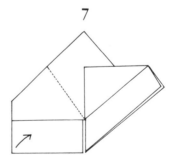

Swing the left flap over to cover the right flap, as in 8.

8

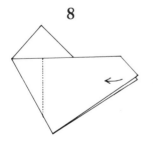

Swing the top flap to the left along the dotted line, as in 9.

9

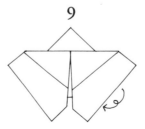

Turn the napkin over for the finished butterfly, as in 10.

10

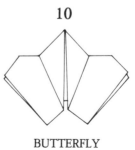

BUTTERFLY

BOAT WITH SAILS

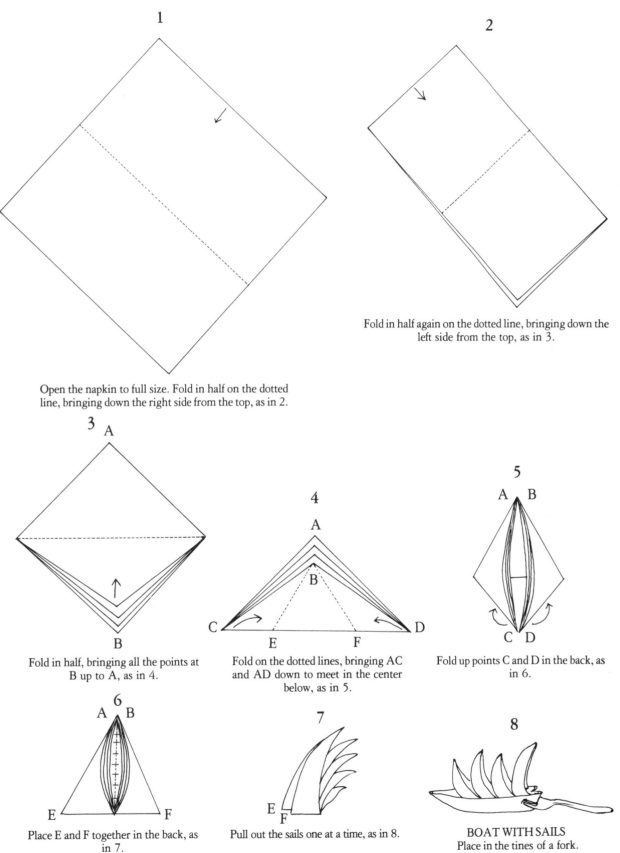

1

Open the napkin to full size. Fold in half on the dotted line, bringing down the right side from the top, as in 2.

2

Fold in half again on the dotted line, bringing down the left side from the top, as in 3.

3

Fold in half, bringing all the points at B up to A, as in 4.

4

Fold on the dotted lines, bringing AC and AD down to meet in the center below, as in 5.

5

Fold up points C and D in the back, as in 6.

6

Place E and F together in the back, as in 7.

7

Pull out the sails one at a time, as in 8.

8

BOAT WITH SAILS
Place in the tines of a fork.

NOTE: This napkin is folded facing you, without ever turning it.

39

BOOT OR LADY'S SLIPPER

1

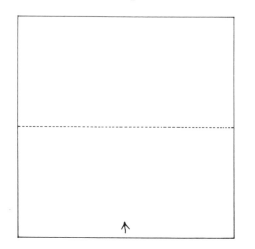

Open the napkin to full size. Fold in half on the dotted line, bringing the bottom edge to the top, as in 2.

2

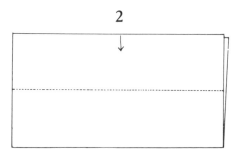

Fold in half again on the dotted line, bringing both top edges down to the bottom crease, as in 3.

3

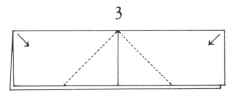
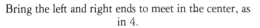

Bring the left and right ends to meet in the center, as in 4.

4

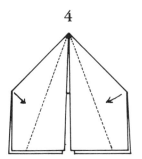

Fold on the dotted lines, again bringing the left and right to the center, as in 5.

5

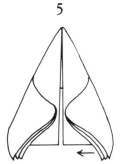

Bring the right half over the left half and place horizontally with the point at the left, the tails at the right, and the opening at the bottom, as in 6.

6

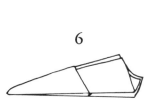

There are two tails on the right. Lift up the top tail and tuck it under and up, as in 7.

7

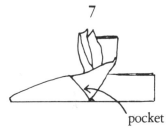

The lower tail must be made narrow in order to tuck it into the pocket; do this by folding the top down and the bottom up as in 8.

8

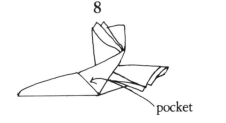

Put the folded tail into the pocket to lock. Stand up, as in 9, and turn up the point of the boot.

9

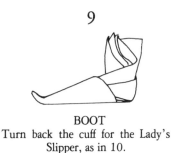

BOOT
Turn back the cuff for the Lady's Slipper, as in 10.

10

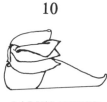

LADY'S SLIPPER

NOTE: Use a red or green napkin to make an Elf's boot for Christmas and a brown napkin to make a cowboy's boot.

RABBIT

1

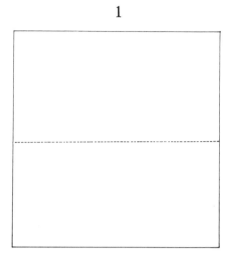

Open the napkin to full size. Fold in half on the dotted line, bringing the top edge to the bottom edge, as in 2.

2

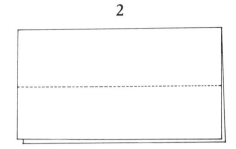

Fold in half again on the dotted line, bringing the top fold to the bottom, as in 3.

3

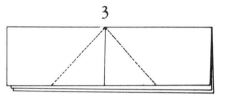

Find the center by bringing the two sides together, creasing and opening again. Bring the right and left sides to meet in the center, as in 4.

4

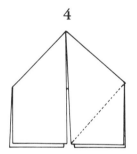

Lay the bottom right raw edges on the middle crease, as in 5.

5

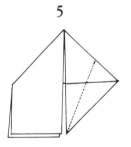

Fold the right side in half on the dotted line, bringing the right to the center and making an ear, as in 6.

6

Repeat 4 and 5 on the left side to get 7.

7

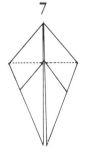

Fold the top point down in the back, as in 8.

8

pocket

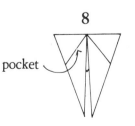

Tuck the right point into the left pocket, as in 9.

9

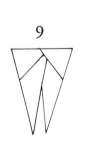

Turn upside down for the finished rabbit, as in 10.

10

RABBIT